UnPhased

BALANCING FINANCE AND EMOTION

KEITH MOONEY
JOE LYONS

Unphased, Balancing Finance and Emotion

ISBN 978-1506-905-50-1 HC/JAC
ISBN 978-1506-905-33-4 PBK
ISBN 978-1506-905-34-1 EBK

LCCN 2017960692

December 2017

Published and Distributed by
First Edition Design Publishing, Inc.
P.O. Box 20217, Sarasota, FL 34276-3217
www.firsteditiondesignpublishing.com

We dedicate this book to our families, mentors, clients, and staff members. Without all of your support through the last twenty plus years, the journey would have been much less enjoyable and rewarding.

Foreword

If you've ever been at home after dark and suffered a power outage, you know what an intimidating experience it can be. Your brightly lit house is suddenly plunged into complete darkness, leaving you groping for candles or a flashlight.

For many individuals, the specter of approaching retirement can be similarly intimidating.

Will your health hold out? Will your family stay together? Will they be able to take care of their aging parents? For many, the most pressing and concerning question is whether there will be enough money to pay for all the known and unknown expenses that inevitably arise during retirement, now that they no longer have a source of full time income.

Given the urgency and importance of these decisions, it's understandable that most families seek out professional help in navigating family and financial issues in retirement. But who can they trust to guide them through this perilous chapter of their life? Who can they rely on to help them plan the rest of their life? Who will be at the helm to help them navigate to their desired destination?

As a representative of one of the largest investment management organizations in the country, I was in a unique position to meet and observe the practices of thousands of financial advisors throughout the Midwest. It was rare to associate with and to work side by side with a tandem of financial advisors as professional as Keith and Joe. It was an honor to support their career efforts for over 20 years.

When I think of Keith and Joe, what comes to mind is their work ethic. They are committed to excellence and to constant improvement in their craft. They serve their clients with the most forward thinking, client centric best practices in the industry. They never take short cuts; they always act in their clients' best interests.

They are creative problem solvers, not salesmen. They are always looking for the most beneficial solutions to even the most complex problems. And they do this with great humility, without any need to bring attention or promotion to themselves. They talk to their clients — not at their clients.

I never found them to be distracted by the schemes that emerge in the financial industry. They stayed disciplined and dedicated to providing the highest quality, personalized solutions for their clients.

In this book, Keith and Joe guide readers through the financial scenarios readers are likely to encounter as they transition through the phases of their financial life, issues virtually everyone experiences but may not be aware of as they are happening. The potential solutions to these challenges are detailed to help readers avoid the financial storms that prevent so many from reaching their safe harbor.

Steven Reitman
Retired Senior VP of American Funds Distributors

Introduction

The Three Phases of Your Financial Life

Over the past twenty plus years, we've helped a lot of people find solutions to their financial problems and investment considerations. Invariably, the underpinning for the solutions is a sound financial plan.

Throughout this book, we're going to walk you through a variety of different financial scenarios. Not every person experiences every situation, of course, but everyone does go through three distinct phases of their financial life. We've segmented these phases by age but do not intend to categorize people simply by how many years they have been walking around on the planet.

We're using the term "phases" to illustrate the different points of life each person goes through and what typically happens during those phases — financially, personally and emotionally. The phases provide a depiction of what we think most people go through, based on our professional experience. Everyone experiences these phases one way or another but not everyone realizes they are going through them.

Don't be put off if the terms don't seem to apply exactly to your circumstances or your period of life. Your authors are a good example of how two people can be at a similar time of life but encounter dramatically different personal and financial challenges. We are approximately the same age but Keith is married with three children: the oldest is a college junior, the middle child a high school senior, the youngest a high school junior. Joe is also married but with one child, a two-year old toddler.

The focus of our message is to help you find value, confidence and reassurance, regardless of your phase of life. There are solutions to the challenges in each phase. We hope to guide you through your phases and help you avoid making the needless mistakes that jeopardize the financial and psychological wellbeing of the people who make them.

Phase One: Young Achievers

Young achievers are people in their early 20's to mid-40's. They are usually high-income earners who have not yet become rich: employees with a healthy 401k; managers or executives with both a 401k and stock options; entrepreneurs busy building a business; legal, financial or healthcare professionals building a practice; dual-income couples; public education or nonprofit employees with 403b plans; government workers and civil service workers with employer-sponsored 457b plans; possibly someone working in sales or the technology industry making an extraordinary high income.

They may have children whose education requires funding. They may be looking to buy their first home or already have a substantial mortgage. These are busy people in the early to mid-stages of their careers, typically lacking a long-term financial plan. Despite their education or success, they may not be overly sophisticated when it comes to their finances. They need help clarifying their financial position, someone to put all the disparate pieces of their portfolio together.

Phase Two: Accumulators

Accumulators represent the second phase, which begins in the mid-forties. These are people who have accumulated significant wealth — anywhere from 500,000 to several million dollars or more — but are unsure whether they are actually rich. They have amassed a broad array of personal assets and investment products but, like their young achiever counterparts, typically lack a formal plan. The financial products they own may not be complementary. If their children have completed their education and are out of the house, their expenses are typically lower and they have more money to save and invest. On the other hand, if they are still paying for their kids schooling or if their kids have graduated but can't find work and are still living at home, or if they are trying to help their kids get started in life by funding advanced education, buying a first home or starting a business, their expenses probably haven't lowered; indeed, they may have escalated and the parents are beginning to wonder if they will ever be able to start saving more for their own future. Retirement is on the horizon but, depending on their financial circumstances, they may or may not be thinking much about it.

Accumulators are often conflicted. They don't know if they have amassed enough wealth to be comfortable, much less rich. People tell them they are rich but they don't feel like it. We've known people with ten million dollar portfolios who don't feel wealthy because they socialize with people who have twenty or thirty million dollar portfolios. They're rich but they don't think they are. It's often a matter of perception. Regardless of size, their portfolios tend to be a jumble of elements acquired over the years, and they lack a solid financial plan for moving on to the next stage of their financial life.

Phase Three: Transitionals

Phase three begins in the years just prior to retirement. At this point, transitionals who saved and invested wisely have stockpiled well in excess of what they will need for a fulfilling retirement...yet they have some nagging doubts about the future. They wrestle with the reality that once they decide to retire, they won't be doing what they have done so well for the past few decades: earn money. A slew of emotions arise as they confront having to transition from earning money to spending it. For highly successful people who have dedicated themselves to career achievement and the accumulation of wealth, the recognition that they will no longer have that stimulation and sense of accomplishment in their lives can be emotionally debilitating. This realization rarely occurs until people reach the transitional phase.

Many transitionals find they are unable to simply retire. It often has less to do with money than the inability to extricate themselves from a lifetime of being productive. It's highly unusual for our clients to merely stop working and enter retirement. Most continue working in some capacity for at least a few years, either in a consulting role related to their industry or profession, or part-time activity in a field of interest. Despite typically having more than enough to retire comfortably, many people continue working in some capacity for a few years to supplement their income. In particular, we see executives and professionals — people earning a couple hundred thousand dollars a year or more — doing some sort of consulting during the early years of retirement. It satisfies their need to continue feeling productive and helps make the transition into full retirement easier to embrace. For those earning less, working in retirement is as much a financial necessity as one of satisfaction.

In any case, it's just plain hard to suddenly shift from being a breadwinner to pulling the trigger and sliding into retirement. The emotions and uncertainty associated with making the transition are difficult to relate to until you actually experience them.

Of course, the fear of outliving one's money often looms in the background. Even though, in many cases, retirees have ample financial reserves, they remain anxious, worried if they will have enough.

Whatever phase you might be in right now, when it comes to your financial future, it's not what you know; it's what you don't know. As advisors, we experience the same emotions and concerns you do. The difference is because we deal with our client's feelings every day, we are acutely aware of those feelings, whereas like many of our clients, you may not recognize that you are experiencing them.

You can fight the dragon or hide from it. We've been there many times. We're writing this book because we believe we can help you make seamless transitions through the various financial phases of your life.

Chapter One

Phase 1: Young Achievers

Millennials (ages 18-34) now number over 80 million and have surpassed Baby Boomers as the nation's largest living generation.[1] The immense size of this population segment portends some significant changes for our country. They are a generation raised with and immersed in technology. As a group, they are both highly educated and highly unemployed.

According to a Wall Street Journal/NBC News poll, a record high 76% of adult Americans lack the confidence that their children's generation will have a better life than they do. Paul Taylor, author of *The New America* and executive vice president of the Pew Research Center says, "Younger people in their 20s and early 30s are at risk of becoming the first generation in history to have a lower standard of living than their parents."

According to the 2015 Pew Research survey, Millennials are the first generation in the modern era to have higher levels of student loan debt, poverty and unemployment than their two immediate predecessor generations at the same stage of life,

In addition, Millennials will be the first generation to face retirement without the benefit of employer guaranteed pensions, since replaced by personal savings in the form of 401k accounts. Throw in the question of whether Social Security and Medicare benefits will still exist in some viable form by the time they retire, and it's apparent that this generation faces some unique financial challenges. Once the entire Baby Boomer generation has moved into retirement, Social Security will only be able to pay 77% of promised benefits, according to a 2013 report by Congressional representatives Robert Reischauer and Charles Blahous. Fifty years ago, the poorest group in America was the elderly; today it is the young.

Obviously, Millennials face some staggering financial and lifestyle challenges. Despite these obstacles, Millennials save an average of 7.5% of their income, a higher increase in savings rate than any other generation, per a 2015 study by Fidelity Investments. A separate study by Bankrate indicates 29% of Millennials are saving more than 10% of their incomes.

Another unique aspect of the Millennial generation is the postponement of marriage. Since 1950, the median age at which both men and women have married has steadily increased. In 1950, men first married at age 22.8 and women at age 20.3. By 2013 the median marriage age increased by more than 6 years for both genders, reaching 29.0 and 26.6 for men and women respectively. As more young adults delay marriage, the fraction who are currently married has fallen. Millennials have continued on this path and are marrying later, with more of them remaining unmarried in their 20s. In 2013, only 30 percent of 20 to 34 year-olds were married, compared to 77 percent in 1960.[2]

Clark University Psychology Professor Jeffrey Arnett has studied Millennials for more than two decades. He takes issue with the media's often disparaging portrayal of Millennials as freeloaders living off their parents. "People call them lazy, and I just laugh," says Arnett. "Look around you: People who are working these low-level service jobs in the Starbucks or the retail store or waiting your tables, they're almost all emerging adults, and they're often ... going to school as well as working, and so it's really not fair to call them, as a generation, lazy. They're anything but."[3]

Arnett adds that rising college costs, student loan debt and urban living expenses all contribute to Millennials' financial strains. They must work while going to school and, because of economic realities, may need to live at home or rely on parents financially. When Mom and Dad support their 20-something children, they are continuing a long tradition of familial interdependence, something Arnett views as healthy.[4]

On the other hand, there are a large number of Millennials who debunk the stereotype of the unemployed, living-at-home-with-the-folks Millennial. They have achieved significant financial success at a much earlier age than their generational predecessors. Smart, talented and ambitious, many have accumulated substantial investable assets. Yet despite their nascent financial clout, many admit they are less than confident about their ability to effectively manage their money.

Merrill Lynch conducted a *Young High Net Worth Insights Survey* among affluent Millennials, including both those who inherited most of their wealth as well as those who acquired it through entrepreneurial ventures or by working their way up at lucrative jobs. While each had investable assets of at least $1 million, very few described themselves as having a high level of knowledge regarding financial and investment matters. The Millennials in the survey did not come across as entitled, disengaged or enthralled by instant gratification. Instead, the data portrays a group who are very much oriented toward the future, and who have a strong sense of responsibility, whether to their families or their communities or society in general.

These young people aren't rebelling against the traditional investment approaches advocated by their parents — not only do most say they would have no objection to using their parents' financial advisors, they are also most likely to describe their investment philosophy as "buy and hold." They aren't turning to their friends and peers in their digitally managed social networks for investment guidance and don't uniformly spurn professional advice. To the contrary, eager to learn, they seem to value expertise wherever they can find it.

Our own experience working with Millennials supports this conclusion. While motivated and exceptional, many concede they are not well prepared when it comes to managing their financial assets. Here are some examples among the many Millennials we have helped pursue financial stability over the years.

Pam, 26, is an example of a Millennial whose plans don't fit the typical template of someone her age. Just getting started on her career in advertising, Pam already knows that she wants to retire early and do charitable work overseas. She questioned whether her dream was possible, and if so, how she could make it happen. What were the obstacles? Was she overlooking anything? We kind of design a couple phases in our life, Pam wants to add another one.

Pam was fully committed to her goal and had a definite timeline in mind for achieving it. Interestingly, her concerns were not as much about having enough money to do it but more about the timing. She told us, "I want to retire from work, move overseas and do charitable work when I'm 45. At that age, I'll be old enough to have acquired sufficient knowledge for the work, but still young enough not to be intimidated by the challenge. I want to spend 15-20 years doing the charitable work, then return to the U.S. and retire here."

What Pam needed was for us to provide the logistical support for her plan. She wanted us to work the numbers backwards and tell her how much she needs to save, where it needs to be invested in order to pursue the returns she needs to get her to her goal.

Pam is an example of the non-stereotypical Millennial. Not many people plan to devote 20 years out of the middle of their life to a goal while they are still in their twenties.

George is 36 and an executive in the insurance industry. He's worked for three different companies in the past ten years. He had vested stock options with two startups that were subsequently sold. He also had 401k plans with two of the firms. George now has a phantom stock plan[5] with his current employer, a company that is also likely to be acquired in the next couple of years. His wife had a professional career but quit when she gave birth to the first of the couple's three children.

On paper, the couple is worth a lot of money. George was accumulating all these assets but wasn't sure how they fit together and what it meant to him long term. Long term, George believes his financial picture has potential but short term, the couple struggles to meet their overhead expenses with three children under age six. We were able to help him understand how to align their finances with both their short and long term plans. We assessed the value of his stock options and provided explanation. George is typical of the successful Millennial who is asset rich but lacking adequate cash flow.

Frank is a fellow with problems most people would love to have. He's 37 and owner of a successful IT business he started during his college years. Recently married, he and his new bride are about to start a family. Our conversations with Frank are centered around taxes, facilitating a smooth business transition and early retirement. Frank is another example of a Millennial who is worth a lot of money on paper, but does not have a lot of tangible assets aside from his business holdings. Not many people create a viable business while still in college or become multimillionaires by the time they're 30. But Frank is a workaholic. He loves what he does and continues to build a business empire, but managing his personal finances are an extraneous activity for him. His primary concern is paying several hundred thousand dollars in year in taxes. He came to us to see if he could find a way to make better use of the money. Additional conversations now center around how long he really wants to continue working and whether taking an early retirement and retaining partial ownership of the business might make sense. That brings into focus the issue of business transition and employees. Does he want to surround himself with people capable of taking over the business?

In Frank's case, financial considerations are not about whether his money is going to last — that's a given — but rather planning how long he wants to continue the arduous schedule of running the business as opposed to spending time raising his soon-to-be family. It's a decision he needs someone to help him think about because he is so wrapped up in his work that he doesn't think about what's down the road.

Millennials are singular in many ways. Many saw their parents struggle at different times and want to avoid that situation. Their parents went through the dotcom bust of 2000 and the real estate and market meltdown of 2008. Their Baby Boomer parents may have been laid off as the economy struggled, couldn't find a replacement job or were forced into part time work and a delayed retirement. Millennials may enjoy their time away from work more than previous generations but they want to be prepared for unexpected economic or financial disruption. However, they procrastinate and the years tick by. All of a sudden, they're 45 and without a plan. Now they have to catch up.

Youth is when you blame all your troubles on your parents; maturity is when you learn that everything is the fault of the younger generation.

Anonymous

Chapter Two

Phase 2: Accumulators

We recently met with a middle-aged man who owned and managed a successful distribution business. "I've spent the past 20-plus years growing the firm into a highly profitable operation," he began. "My son joined the business after graduating college a few years ago and now he is close to being ready to take over the day-to-day operations. For the first time, I'm able to shift some of my attention from the business to my personal finances."

He continued, "I've been saving for retirement, of course, however I've also accumulated a lot of other investments and financial products that my advisors told me I need, except I really don't know how they all fit together. I feel like I've done the right thing by following their advice but I don't feel like I'm in control of what's happening with all these different pieces. They all tell me I'm doing fine although I don't really have a plan. All my personal stuff just sort of happened while I was building the business."

His story is not an uncommon one. We regularly encounter individuals and couples with thriving careers and an array of uncorrelated personal investments, insurance and other assets. They've been so busy making money and accumulating assets, they haven't thought much about how to integrate all those assets into a comprehensive financial plan.

As children, most of us were taught that if we worked hard and saved our money, everything else would take care of itself. If you were fortunate and your parents passed on meaningful values and a vigorous work ethic, you probably enjoy a satisfying life, relish what you do for a living and look forward to a fulfilling retirement.

As someone who has accumulated significant assets — whether as a corporate executive, business owner, professional or successful whatever — most of the decisions you've made have been good ones. You've done a lot of things well and that burgeoning investment portfolio has you thinking it may be time to seek a more refined financial resource to help manage what you have built and guide you through your eventual transition into retirement.

If you have been managing your own money, you might feel a twinge of unease as your portfolio has swelled to impressive proportions and become an increasingly imposing responsibility. Given the time commitment, you may also question whether it still makes sense for you to be the sole captain of your financial ship. If you have been getting advisory help, it may be the agent from whom you purchased your first life insurance policy, your longtime stockbroker or an advisor recommended by a friend or colleague. Their services may have been adequate while you were in the earlier stages of creating your asset base but you sense you now need a higher level of financial expertise or more sophisticated investment approach.

In either case, you probably have accumulated a variety of financial products but lack a cohesive strategy that unifies your investments and provides critical diversifi-cation. You suspect you are ready for a more personal working relationship with an experienced advisor in whom you feel complete trust and confidence. Someone who is part of a knowledgeable advisory team dedicated to your best interests and to helping guide you into the future.

You may not yet know who that professional may be or exactly what you need, but you know you are ready for something better, something more holistic that addresses both your financial and emotional needs. You wonder if you have sufficient assets to engage advisory help that meets those more demanding requirements; someone who listens well and can create a financial roadmap that provides confidence and reassurance as you move forward toward retirement; someone to help guide you the rest of the way.

Chapter Three

Phase 3: Transitionals

The professional success and financial stability you've achieved are the foundation for your retirement. You've worked hard, saved and foregone some of life's luxuries in the hopes that you will have the necessary income to do the things you love most and not have to worry about outliving your money.

The assets you've accumulated should be sufficient to retire comfortably, but with the average life expectancy now at a record high of 78 8 years,[6] there is always the potential for outliving your money. The problem with average life expectancy statistics is that they reflect the entire population, not necessarily you as an individual. Your retirement might be 5 years or 50 years. It's different for everybody. Given the advances in medical technology and consumer knowledge, it's not uncommon for people to live well into their nineties or even beyond. An amazing thought is that depending on when you retire, you might spend more years in retirement than you did working.

You know how it feels to work for three, four or five decades, but it's hard to imagine what it would be like to be retired and no longer working for that long. As a society, we don't have a lot of experience or data on 40 or 50-year retirements; it's a phenomenon we are just beginning to examine.

Many people find it psychologically difficult to make the transition from earning and saving money to withdrawing and spending it. Some hesitate to retire because they're uneasy about no longer making money. Others simply find it hard to "let go" when retirement looms.

The day you retire, you have this mountain of money you've worked decades to amass. You want to build a protective moat around it, but your advisor tells you that you have to start spending it, depleting your assets in order to generate income. Hearing this twists you in circles. You think, "This is contrary to everything I learned from an early age; contrary to everything I have been doing for the past half century. My folks taught me to work hard, live within my means and save my money. Now all of a sudden, all that financial advice is being thrown out the window. I'm expected to quit working, quit saving money and spend what I have. It just doesn't feel right."

We met with a highly accomplished professional about to retire with liquid assets in excess of two million dollars. Several of his friends enjoyed similar financial standing and so his wealth was not apparent. Financially speaking, he considered himself "just one of the guys." When we mentioned the word "plan," it struck a chord with him. Despite his wealth, he didn't have even the semblance of a plan. We evaluated his financial position and produced an analysis. He looked at it and asked us, "So am I rich or not?"

His reaction is not unusual. Unless someone has reached a plateau above a hundred million dollars, they don't believe they are rich. They've done everything right but they still have doubts whether they will be all right.

It's a new paradigm, calling for a completely different strategy for handling your money. It's tough, and no matter how smart, organized or knowledgeable you are about financial matters, you realize that once retired, if you mess up, you can't go back and start over again. If the market drops and your retirement portfolio takes a hit during your working years, you may not be happy about it but you figure that the worst case scenario is you'll have to work a while longer before retiring. The first time the market goes into free fall after you retire, it's a completely different experience. Seeing 15, 20 or 30 percent of your portfolio disappear in just a few days or weeks can be emotionally devastating when you're retired. Your first thought is, "I'm screwed. I can't go back to my old career; no one will pay me what I used to earn because there are plenty of younger guys willing to work for less. I'm damn sure not going to go work at Home Depot for 12 dollars an hour."

All these thoughts rattle around in your head and won't go away. You can't sleep, worried that another market swoon will mean drastically changing your lifestyle, giving up the things you dreamed about doing in retirement. This isn't what you expected when you were putting money aside for retirement all those years.

The control you've felt all your life making business decisions and being in charge is suddenly gone. You may feel as though you've lost much of your identity. You are no longer a mover and shaker. You are now just another retired person, watching your retirement capital shrink and feeling helpless.

"The harder you work, the harder it is to surrender."
Vince Lombardi

Mounting Stress

When you were younger, retirement was a remote concept. You attended to the necessary financial provisions but gave little thought to the psychological ramifications of retirement. As you grow nearer to retirement, a sense of anxiety begins to arise. The unknown can be intimidating.

In his paper, "Avoiding The Stress Of Retirement," psychologist Dr. Gerald Fishkin talks about the "Sense of foreboding that may set in as retirement nears, when people confront the reality that their working years are coming to an end. Many regard retirement in much the same context as death, that is, the end of productive life. This causes them to avoid discussing or even thinking rationally about their retirement, let alone plan for how to deal with it. This only serves to make the underlying stress more severe than it need be."

For some, retirement is facing the death of their careers. They actually experience what psychiatrist Elisabeth Kübler-Ross identified as the model for the five stages of bereavement: denial, anger, bargaining, depression or sadness and finally, acceptance.

According to psychologist Kris Ludwigsen, "Work is the primary source of identity for many people and absorbs their best energies and creativity, so retirement is a major transition. Many people give so much of themselves to their work that they don't have the time or energy to develop other interests, and they are left adrift in retirement. Their job gave their life meaning, and not having that is the worst stress of all. That's why some people want to continue to work as long as they can."[7]

A client of ours was an executive in the communications industry. He postponed retirement several times because each year, he received a substantial bonus as part of his compensation package. He and his wife always had "just one more" bill to pay off or one more major purchase to make and so, his plan to retire kept getting postponed. Each year during this period, we assured him that he had more than enough money to retire comfortably and be able do all the things he and his wife planned to do. But the lure of that extra money and, I believe, his hesitancy to retire because it meant no longer being an "earner" wouldn't allow him to pull the trigger. Now, a few years later and thoroughly enjoying his post-working years, he looked back on those delays and laughingly told us wished he had taken our advice and retired earlier.

In all the years we have been advising clients, neither of us ever had a retiree say that he or she wished they could have gone to one more meeting or had to meet one more deadline. They almost all say they wish they had retired sooner.

The Perceived Safety Net

It's natural to question the future as you make your transition into retirement. When you were working, you felt as though you had a safety net. It may have been more perception than reality but it gave you peace of mind. You looked at money and investing a certain way all your adult life but suddenly you see it differently. If you had sound financial advice while working, you learned that market dips can provide opportunities to accumulate more shares, commonly called dollar averaging[8]. Now in retirement, market volatility becomes a different animal for you. You're no longer able to make up investment losses with personal income. Volatility has become the enemy. You shudder at the thought of another 2008 gutting your investment portfolio.

The First Drop

Most of your decisions have been good ones. You now have to be even more cautious to protect yourself from making bad transition decisions. The first serious market correction you go through can be traumatic. Your perspective is so much different now that you are no longer working. The tendency is to overreact to that first drop and make flawed decisions because you are now living off your assets. You must be emotionally prepared for your retirement's first market plunge. It will come.

We have been helping clients prepare for retirement long enough to know that when that first market downturn occurs, we have to be ready to reassure and guide them through it. Their angst is a normal response. That's when the value of the long-standing advisory relationship really becomes evident. What is equally fascinating is when clients retired for 15 or 20 years' experience their third or fourth market dip, it is not as impactful. If we call to see how they are doing, they ask why we are even talking about it? But that first market plunge is a big deal for everyone.

Financial Marketing

When someone becomes a client just prior to or after retiring, we often find they recently purchased some type of financial product, ostensibly to meet their retirement needs. What they rarely have in place is a retirement plan. Typically, they bought something that sounded good as opposed to first formulating a plan, then finding a product that would fulfill the plan's requirements.

We try to make the product work for them but sometimes it's impossible. The financial industry is far more oriented to marketing than planning. For financial product manufacturers and brokers, selling is far more lucrative than planning. It can lead to people buying the wrong thing at the wrong time.

Risk Management Adjustment

During your working years, risk management involves having sufficient assets to pay off debts and provide income for your family should you become disabled or die prematurely. Once you reach retirement, risk management becomes an issue for your investments. You likely have enough assets to provide for loved ones should you die prematurely but what if you get sick and need nursing home care? How much will health insurance and long-term care protection cost? How will you safeguard assets for your spouse? If one of you gets dementia, will there be sufficient funds to protect the other? There are lots of questions that need answers.

Another consideration is the emotional aspect of risk management: guarding against poor decisions. Retirees often feel the need to manage their money more closely. They can't resist spending time each day nervously watching and overreacting to every minor twitch in the markets. They end up over-managing their portfolio, hovering over it like anxious parents watching their children cross a busy street for the first time.

Everyone says they are okay with risk until it happens. Then their risk tolerance evaporates. An advisor's value sometimes is not apparent until you need someone to talk you off the ledge after a market disaster. We may be somewhat biased, being advisors, but so little is said about the importance of having a trusted relationship when things go sideways. We are an underpaid resource when that happens.

Retirement should be one of the best parts of your life, if not the best. If you have an established relationship with an advisor you trust and a solid retirement plan, you will be better equipped to avoid the temptation to overreact to bad news or start to micro-manage your portfolio. It's a wonderful feeling to know you have a plan and a person to help get you through the rough times. You can live in the present, remain confident and go do the things you enjoy. That's what we all hope for in our retirement, isn't it?

"You know you're getting old when you stoop to tie your shoelaces and wonder what else you could do while you're down there."

George Burns

Chapter Four

Investment Traps

"The broker said the stock was poised to move. Silly me, I thought he meant up."
Anonymous

The long road to a successful retirement is hardly a superhighway. Potholes, traffic and detours abound in the form of behavioral biases, transition stress and mass media misinformation. Avoiding the distractions and debris that threatens your retirement plan calls for an accurate navigation system and some serious driving skills.

But even alert drivers with the right directions get sidetracked because they chose the wrong vehicle. It's hard to count the number of times new clients have come to us having purchased an investment product mismatched with their financial goals. In most cases, it's not that the product is inherently bad but rather that it simply isn't aligned with what they are trying to accomplish. They bought a product before they had a plan. They chose the vehicle for their retirement trip without first evaluating the road conditions and their destination.

Financial products are sold, not bought. The fact that this occurs so frequently is a testament to the effectiveness of the people involved in marketing and selling financial products, and whose efforts may be disguised as investment advice. It's one reason why having a relationship with an advisor you can trust is so important.

Square Peg and Round Hole

More retirements are sidetracked by choosing the wrong investment products or strategy than by inferior investment performance. Even supposedly sophisticated investors can end up with financial products that fail to align with their long-term goals, fall within the parameters of their risk tolerance, mesh with their existing asset allocation or have adequate liquidity.

There are powerful forces supporting these products. The insurance industry, banks selling CDs, brokerage houses selling equities and mutual funds, precious metals firms and day trading services all spend untold amounts each year promoting their products. A compliant mass media contributes to the misinformation by sponsoring 24/7 financial news that promotes a hectic environment and continuous trading, as well as being funded by the huge advertising budgets of product manufacturers.

The other day, I saw a TV commercial that begins, "We've just uncovered a horde of previously uncirculated gold coins...." I recall seeing that same commercial for 10 or 15 years. Obviously, it continues to draw buyers, a testament to the advertising mantra that the audience is a moving target.

The financial services industry is evolving but for decades the mentality has been one of moving product versus what best meets the needs of each client's goals and capacity for risk. The whole process is backwards. The industry should be promoting the concept of first putting a plan in place and then finding appropriate products to address the goals of the plan. It should be doing what we did years ago: deciding whether to become stockbrokers selling products or advisors helping people work towards a satisfying retirement.

You can pick virtually any financial product and find advocates who say it's good or dissidents who say the opposite. Take real estate, for example:

We know an elderly man, Sam, who has invested every dollar available in land and life insurance throughout his life. His father promoted those two items and drilled the belief into his son from an early age. Now in his eighties, Sam has amassed what would be an impressive real estate portfolio, but having all his money tied up in non-liquid assets has left the couple strapped for cash. They now have to scrape by every year, barely managing to pay the real estate property taxes and the premiums on Sam's life insurance policy. Sam recently developed dementia and his wife doesn't know how she will be able to keep the household together without money.

This illustrates the importance of avoiding falling in love with a single asset. Which brings us to our first myth:

You Can't Lose Money In Real Estate

Many regard real estate as a tangible investment that can't lose money, but as we have seen over the past decade, that's not the case. Even before the catastrophic plunge of 2008, many real estate investors had a distorted view of how much profit they were actually earning. After allowing for the costs of marketing and maintaining the property, utilities, insurance, taxes and occupancy, the real rate of return can be far less than they imagined.

Seeing the rent checks arrive every month, investors tend to discount the costs, believing they are ahead of the game, but once all the related expenses are calculated, the money coming in is usually less than the money going out. And that's before you consider the personal time spent painting, repairs and other problems, not to mention the headache of getting a phone call at 2am from a distressed renter whose toilet just overflowed. Compared to a passive investment like equities or a stock fund, owning real estate involves work and having tenants relying on you to solve their problems.

We've both owned investment properties and while there were a couple of years when things where great and we made money, there were also years where we lost our shirts. In conversations with investors about their real estate, we often find they don't take into consideration all of the true costs, time investment and emotional expenditure when estimating their profit or loss. Of course, real estate is a tangible asset, something investors can see and feel good about owning. Perhaps that's why they tend to be more emotionally attached to real estate than other assets. But investors also have something in common with gamblers. They rarely talk about losses; they only want you to know about the times they won. You won't hear them talk about taking time off from work and sitting in their car, waiting for the HVAC repairman to show up and fix a broken air conditioning unit, or the lost income while the property was vacant for two months last year.

Advancing age is another issue, both for the properties and the investor. While upkeep costs tend to increase as a property ages, the ability of an investor to control costs by personally taking care of painting, replacing broken cabinets and other maintenance issues diminishes with age. Climbing a ladder to change light bulbs or clean the debris out of the gutters is one thing when you are 50; it's quite another when you are 75. Suddenly, you have to pay for minor repairs you were previously able to handle yourself.

> *"The financial crisis of 2008 was not caused by investment banks betting against the housing market in 2007. It was caused by the fact that too few investors — including all the big investment banks — bet too heavily on the housing market in the years before 2007."*
>
> James Surowiecki

Another widely misunderstood and misapplied product is annuities. We've seen people purchase annuities to fund their children's college education, which is not their intended use, given the 10% additional penalty tax on distributions prior to age 59½. Annuities are not for college; they are for retirement. Annuities, like many other investment products, are not inherently good or bad, despite the vociferous opinions both pro and con. It's how they are used that determines their merit.

Financial marketer Ken Fisher opens a commercial by saying, "I hate annuities and you should too," which leads us to another myth:

Annuities are a Bad Investment

Given the broad array of annuities, the simplification that they are all bad or good is ridiculous. Like any other financial product, they can be appropriate or not, depending on the individual's circumstances and the type of annuity.

Essentially, annuities are long-term investment vehicles designed for retirement purposes. Some are designed to create an income stream, like a pension or Social Security. Some are used to generate growth and may offer additional benefits. Annuities are contracts between an investor and, typically, an insurance company. They are complex products with a lot of moving parts, and should be carefully evaluated as to the intended use. Guarantees are based on the claims paying ability of the issuing company. As with any investment, it's unwise to tie up a disproportionate amount of your money in any single investment, regardless of its rate of return, investment potential or the circumstances involved. Annuities can be a piece of the puzzle but you must be wary of having too much of your portfolio wrapped up in long-term investments, such as annuities with 15 or 20 year surrender charges.

In our opinion, they should not be purchased without the counsel of an advisor with fiduciary responsibility. The potential for misapplication or even abuse is always present. Consider the firm that aggressively marketed high fixed income rate annuities to teachers and other members of the education community. What the firm failed to disclose was the fact that upon retirement, investors were not permitted to withdraw their money in a lump sum; they were only permitted to withdraw 10% per year. No matter how long the investment was retained, there would always be a ten-year surrender charge...in essence, a never-ending surrender charge. It's doubtful that many trusting teachers or administrators would have invested in the product had they been told it contained a permanent ten-year surrender charge that meant no matter how long they kept the annuity, they could only get their money out over a ten-year period. Getting access to all their money at one time was virtually impossible without additional costs.

This kind of deceptive practice tends to unfairly taint everyone in an industry and sad to say, is not limited to a single example. A couple decades ago, an insurance company came up with an annuity product to facilitate 401(k) contributions. The product quietly contained an unbelievable 25-year surrender charge!

Conversely, there are reputable companies offering annuities with much more favorable terms, many with provisions that allow investors to withdraw all or any part of their investment at any time without any surrender charges.

So there are as many or more positive results attained with the appropriate annuity products as there are horror stories. Like safe aircraft landings and everyday heroes, you don't hear about them much because they don't make for headline-grabbing news.

When assessing any financial product, particularly those with complex features such as annuities, it's critical to have a comprehensive understanding of the terms and appropriateness of the investment. Again, the need for competent, trustworthy advice is essential. We've dealt with these products many times and, where prudent, have been able to help investors extract themselves through various structured withdrawal plan strategies.

Over the years, the financial industry continually develops new products to catch the eye of investors, much like the new automobile models each autumn. The appeal of something new can be an irresistible attraction.

Some time back, universal life policies gained widespread popularity because of the high rates or return being offered. Many people converted their traditional life insurance policies to universal life policies to secure the higher rates. Unfortunately, a lot of those policies blew up when rates dropped. This is where a trusted advisor can be beneficial.

Another attraction that proved toxic for some investors were the tax breaks offered by limited partnerships. A lot of high-income earners bought into the strategy and later regretted their decision when 1986 legislation eliminated the tax break. In recent years, wealthy investors seeking tax relief turned to oil drilling. With the price of oil now hovering at historic lows, even the tax breaks can't make up for the investment loss.

Here's another myth for you to consider: Gold Protects You From Global Disaster

Advertisements tout the fact that gold has never been worth zero. Gee whiz, what a great recommendation! If you were around at the end of the Jimmy Carter era in 1981, you may recall that interest rates were through the roof. You could purchase a CD paying 14 percent and gold, valued up to $950 an ounce, was rumored to triple or even quadruple in value in a few years. Well, gold sank to half that value and remained in the trough for another 25 years.[9] You don't hear that fact advertised much, do you?

Gold doesn't make or produce anything that adds to its value. Rapid commodity price swings can trigger significant volatility. Gold is advertised as a hedge against inflation, but the only value is if somebody is willing to pay more than you did for it. It's possible the price may go up as the dollar weakens against inflationary pressures, but it's a premise based on greed. If currency ever came to be valued at next to nothing, how much would gold be worth? You're better off spending your money on canned goods. If you're hungry, they taste a lot better than gold.

> *"Gold is a commodity; over the long run, as we look back, it has not been a good investment. You can't look at the intrinsic value of gold as you can a business. Gold doesn't give you cash flow, and, at the end of the day, cash flow is what is important. Gold doesn't give you dividends."*
>
> Michael Lee-Chin

Chapter Five

The Pension Trap

"I had a pension that I was paying into for 27 years... It's now worth less than a Herman Cain endorsement."
Martin Bashir, BBC host

Sometimes, problems arise not because someone sold an investor the wrong product but because the investor didn't have all the information needed to make a sound choice. For retirees receiving a company pension, perhaps the biggest mistake is choosing the wrong pension option.

Consider Frank, who is about to retire. Frank is married and his company pension offers several choices as to how to receive his money:

	Retiree monthly benefit	Survivor monthly benefit
Single life	$2,000	0
Joint and 100% survivor	$1,500	$1,500
Joint and 50% survivor	$1,700	$ 850

Frank can opt for the most frequently chosen option, the joint and 100% survivor. Here he would receive $1,500 a month and when he dies, his wife would continue to receive the full $1,500 monthly. But this option may not always be the best option because while Frank may understandably wish to ensure that his wife receives the maximum benefit after his death, there is a trade off. If Frank's spouse should die first, not only would he have left the extra $500 per month on the table, he would have received nothing in return. This may not be the best insurance policy as anyone can imagine.

With the second option — the joint 50% survivor — Frank receives $1,700 monthly and when he dies, his wife will continue to receive half the benefit, or $850 a month until her death.

The third option — single life — pays the maximum monthly amount of $2,000 but when Frank dies, the pension payments stop and his wife will receive nothing further. This option cannot be exercised without the written consent of the spouse.

If Frank chooses the second or third option and takes less money up front, he is, in effect, using his pension funds to purchase life insurance. It's an inferior life insurance policy because the issuing company must assume everyone is unhealthy, since there is no physical required.

Looking at this proposition from a different perspective, suppose I am an insurance salesman and you are considering your pension options. I suggest you choose the second or third option. You agree. I now tell you that should your wife die first, you're going to continue to pay the insurance premium but there won't be any benefit for you or your deceased wife.

How does that sound?

Not good, but that's what would happen if your wife passes before you do. By taking one of the lower monthly payments, you are exchanging a significant portion of your monthly benefit — in Frank's case, between $300 and $500 monthly — for an insurance policy that pays nothing unless you die before your wife does. Most people who take the lower monthly benefit option don't understand that they are purchasing a life insurance policy with the administrator, and not a very good one in comparison to what you can purchase separately. If they knew it and were in good health, they would probably rethink their choice. Of course, the company's pension administrator is unlikely to mention that critical piece of information.

Given he is in good health, Frank would probably be best off taking the $2,000 monthly pension option and purchasing a life insurance policy on his own. It's important to understand that funding this strategy requires a boring old permanent life insurance policy with fixed premiums that do not go up as you age. If the premiums on such a policy exceed the difference in the pension's monthly benefit options or are simply not manageable, you are better off choosing one of the pension's lower monthly benefits that include insurance. Even if you purchase a ten or fifteen year level payment policy, if you live beyond that, you lose.

Individuals with an existing policy that may have been purchased to cover a need they no longer have — for example a mortgage that has been paid off — might find it has enough cash value to fund or supplement funding of their retirement needs, and may alleviate the need to purchase an additional policy.

For people receiving a company pension, the biggest life insurance policy they're ever going to buy is when they retire. They can buy a policy from the pension fund or buy one on their own. In many instances, the latter is a better choice, assuming the pensioner can qualify for a policy that meets his specific needs. Once the maximum monthly benefit option is chosen, it is irrevocable so the availability and cost of appropriate life insurance must be thoroughly evaluated beforehand. If the retiree qualifies for the insurance coverage he wants, the policy should be issued and the first payment made before executing the strategy of choosing the pension's maximum monthly benefit.

For those in good health, it would be wise to consider purchasing their life insurance policy in advance of retirement, in order to lock in the health and the lower premiums.

We try to make people aware of these issues when we conduct financial seminars on retirement issues. Some years back, as we concluded the session, one of the attendees came up and exclaimed, "Damn, I wish I had met you fellows years ago." He explained that when he retired, he took the joint 100% survivor option, which amounted to roughly $3,000 a month. Five months later, his wife died unexpectedly. At the time we met him, his wife had been dead for six or seven years, so he had already lost a significant amount of money.

We asked him why he chose that option and he said he had asked his firm's HR department which option to choose on his pension. They asked if he was married or single. He said he was married so they told him the 100% survivor option. It turned out to be a horribly expensive mistake. This took place ten years or so ago, so imagine how much he has lost over all that time.

It's essential to make the proper choice when selecting a pension benefit option. No one should make this decision without the help of a competent advisor with meaningful pension experience. Some situations are even more complex, for example, where both the husband and wife work for the same employer and each has their own pension. Here, choosing the right options involves a more complex and coordinated analysis. Some pensions have provisions that are integrated with Social Security benefits, another factor that must be evaluated before choosing a payment option. In circumstances like these, as well as other unique situations, having an advisor who is familiar with the full spectrum of pension circumstances can be indispensable.

Whatever your pension circumstances, get competent professional help before making any decisions.

There is one other pension benefit option we have not discussed: a lump sum payment. The important consideration here is the internal rate of return provided by the investment vehicle. There's a rate of return built in to the pension benefit product. Can you do better with an alternative product? The only way to find out is to dissect the pension investment product to determine the real rate of return, and compare that with other, comparable investment products

There is also the emotional aspect of the lump sum payment to consider. Some people just want to get their money out of the company, fearing it may not be there years down the road. There are numerous horror stories about diminishing pensions.

Pick almost any airline as an example. In one instance, the pilot for a major airline chose to receive a $140,000 annual pension benefit instead of a two million dollar lump sum payment when he retired. Unfortunately, the airline filed for bankruptcy a few years later and his benefit was reduced by almost $100,000 a year!

The U.S. Government's Pension Benefit Guarantee Corporation (PBGC) was established in 1974 to help protect pensioners of companies that go bankrupt. The pension guarantee fund does not guarantee the full benefits, however.

If your pension plan terminates without sufficient cash to pay all benefits, the insurance program of the PBGC will pay you guaranteed benefits up to the pension limits set by law. Profit sharing and 401(k) plans are not covered.

According to the website pbgc.gov, "Your maximum guaranteed amount is based, in part, on your age on the plan termination date (or the date the sponsor entered bankruptcy, if applicable) or, if you were not in pay status on that date, the date you begin receiving benefits from PBGC. Your maximum guaranteed amount also will reflect the age of your designated beneficiary if your benefit provides payments to a survivor."

"I don't want to tell you how much insurance I carry with the Prudential, but all I can say is: when I go, they go too."

Jack Benny

Chapter Six

Fee Fixation

"It's unwise to pay too much, but worse to pay too little. Pay too much and you lose a little money. Pay too little and you sometimes lose everything, because the thing you bought was incapable of doing the thing it was bought to do."
John Ruskin

The media is currently obsessed with investment fees and the financial services industry has followed suit. Critics everywhere are touting index funds and ETFs as the great investment emancipators, mainly because of their low fees. Collectively, there is a huge marketing emphasis, as if lower fees are the principle criteria for evaluating investment performance.

According to a report from the Investment Company Institute, investors poured $148 billion in net new cash flow into index funds in 2014. Over the past seven years, net asset flows into equity index funds and ETFs topped $1 trillion while actively managed funds saw a net outflow of $659 billion. Cash flows into index funds have steadily increased over the past fifteen years:

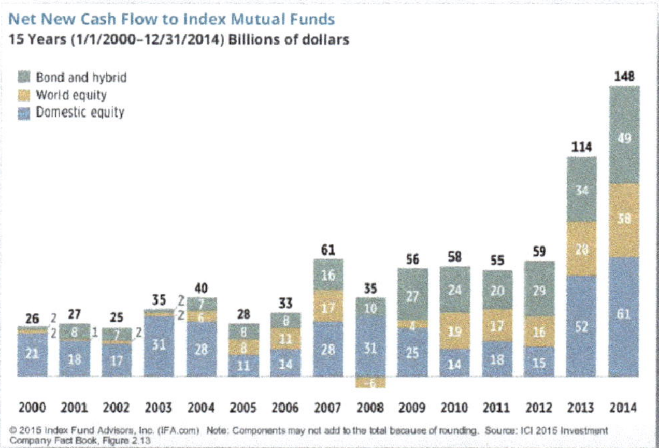

The stampede to index funds continues but to what advantage? When the broad markets take a nosedive, as they did during the first two months of 2015, passive index funds plummeted in lock step.

Once the hype and hoopla about fees has waned and the industry's marketing mavens have moved on to their next "message," this reality remains:

Cost is what you pay; value is what you get.

Myth: Index Funds Outperform Managed Funds

The myth that index funds consistently outperform is untrue and misleading. The S&P 500 was established in

1968 with an initial index value of 96.47. A decade later, at the end of 1978, it languished at 96.11 — right back where it started.

While the press, airwaves and internet are crammed with advertising touting the outperformance of index funds, what is typically not mentioned is that the performance is measured not against comparable investments but against the entire universe of funds. That's like saying I can run faster than half of the world because I am comparing my speed against a population that includes everything from infants to senior citizens. Were I to compare my speed exclusively with males my age, I fear I would probably be in the slowest group. So when index funds make this type of claim, they might be making a comparison with balanced funds, equity income funds and other types of funds which, all being different, can't be measured by the same standards.

Look Beyond Fees

Fees are obviously an important aspect of evaluating investments and some products are burdened with excessive fees that erode investment performance. But the fanatical preoccupation with fees ignores the reality that when the markets tank, stock index fund investors will follow.

Investors must now be reeducated that's it's not just about the fees. As investment advisors, we are conscious of fees. They are one of the elements we always consider when evaluating investments. But the media hysteria that focuses exclusively on fees as the only thing investors should worry about does a great disservice to the investing public. Low fees are advantageous, but not at the cost of overall investment performance. They should not be driving force of investment analysis.

The fee-mania pendulum may be slowing down just a bit. We recently saw where a class action suit was filed against Kraft Foods for its 401(k) investments that were promoted on the basis of having low fees but failed to have the least expensive share class available to participants. No doubt the fact that over the past few years, there have been at least 30 lawsuits against 401(k) plans — alleging fees were too high — contributed to the low-fee emphasis.

Choosing investments based exclusively on fees is perhaps the least sophisticated way of evaluating investments.

Recently, a client of ours decided to transfer $200,000 from his IRA over to a discount brokerage in an effort to save some money on fees. Acting on his own, he transferred the money using a 60-day rollover, where the trustee holding his IRA funds sends the client a check and the client endorses the check over to the custodian. He forgot he had taken a smaller 60-day rollover from his IRA earlier that year. Regulations prohibit making more than one rollover of this type during a calendar year. Making a second rollover becomes a taxable event. The client unwittingly saddled himself with a $60,000 tax bill. Had he notified us of his plan, we could have instructed him to request a direct transfer — as opposed to the 60-day rollover from his IRA. Instead the money would have been transferred from the first trustee to the discount brokerage trustee without our client ever having touched it. There would have been no tax on the transfer and he would be sleeping better as a result of avoiding a large taxable event.

Discount brokers may not have nearly the breadth of experience as an advisor who deals with these types of transactions every day. Even where the broker is aware of the regulations, he is unlikely to ask the client if he has made any previous 60-day rollovers during the year. They may have a specialist on staff somewhere who knows the rules but the clerk who conducts the money transfer is unlikely to have that knowledge or question the transfer.

Sometimes, clients don't recognize the value an advisor provides because they are blinded by a "fee-only" mentality, a perspective that can hinder their goals.

Cost is what you pay; value is what you get.

The idea that either active or passive investment management is always the better choice is the equivalent of believing that the cheapest suit is always the best buy, or the lowest priced car will deliver the best performance. It sounds almost comical when you talk about clothing or automobiles but somehow, the media, the index fund sponsors and even the government are bent on convincing the public that lower fees automatically translate into better returns.

If it were true, why not simply purchase bank CDs or inexpensive Treasury Bills? They certainly qualify as low fee investments. Of course, the returns are paltry. In fact, you would be lucky to keep pace with inflation. On the other hand, you sure as heck will save a little money on fees.

What you should be paying attention to is the net internal rate of return (IRR), the measure of a portfolio or fund's performance after management fees and carried interest have been accounted for. This is important because you can inadvertently purchase high-fee equity funds whose returns are poor if you're not careful.

Myth: Fee Only Advisors Are Better

Fee only advisors are reimbursed by their clients through a billing process and are prohibited from receiving any other compensation. While this is intended to promote the idea that they are offering unbiased advice, in reality, most charge a fee for services. Once you move your assets over, they charge a fee based on the amount of those assets. That's not a fee only arrangement, however; it's a fee-based arrangement. Some advisors charge an additional consulting fee, referring clients to a sister company or a financial product provider with whom they have a reimbursement agreement, which makes them even more money.

Trustworthy advisors disclose their fees with complete transparency. Whether fee only, fee based or commission based, the advisor/client relationship should be based on whatever reimbursement structure best serves the needs of the client. An honest person will always be an honest person no matter how they are paid.

Fees are a consideration but should never be the primary factor when evaluating performance. If you are comparing two portfolios containing the exact same investments being managed in the exact same way, you probably should gravitate to the portfolio with the cheaper fees. But make sure the net IRR for each portfolio is also similar before you make your choice.

Logic tells us it only makes sense to pay higher fees for an investment we believe offers greater profit potential, or to an active manager we trust who has the potential to deliver higher net returns, despite a higher fee.

"Any time an investment company has to spend heavily on advertising, it's probably a bad business in which to invest."

Robert Kiyosaki

Chapter Seven

You Need a Plan

Regardless of what phase you are in, your level of income or career achievements, you need a detailed plan that aggregates all of your financial pieces into a plan that you can follow. In addition to providing clarity about what you already have and a roadmap for where you are going, a financial plan should guide you past the obstacles that might jeopardize your journey. A plan should provide you with the confidence that you won't make any major mistakes due to impulsive or emotionally driven decisions. It should help prevent you from being distracted by the noise from the 24/7 financial media, product marketers and well-intentioned but uninformed friends. It should reduce your stress so you don't have to be thinking about your money every time the market has a hiccup. It should be a source of confidence and reassurance that you are on the right track as you pursue your goals.

It simply makes sense to have a plan in place, a strategy with a qualified professional who can monitor and adjust it for you as you move forward.

"Adventure is just bad planning."
Roald Amundsen

Emotions

A consideration that even the most intelligent investors often overlook is the powerful impact emotions have on their decision-making. Decades of research into behavioral finance reveals the irrefutable connection between our psychological biases and our ability to make sound financial decisions. We'll discuss the importance of recognizing and understanding these biases in the book.

One of the vital components of successful investing is a sound financial plan. Yet we consistently meet people who have such a plan — often an expensively bound volume that has since been relegated to a desk drawer or closet shelf — but it failed to account for the unanticipated events that occur in virtually everyone's life at some point. Illness, divorce, accidents, economic upheaval and other unforeseen challenges will threaten even the most carefully crafted financial plan. As anyone who has served in the military knows, most battle plans are jettisoned once the first shot is fired.

By no means do we suggest that planning is a waste of time, but rather that any financial plan worth paying for must include provisions for the unexpected — the inevitable misfortunes that will test your commitment to stay the course, as well as your ability to resist emotionally driven responses.

For most people, investment success is determined not by what happens to them but by how they react to what happens. That's an important distinction and it relates to the behavioral issues we mentioned. As a result of thousands of years of evolution, our DNA is wired to react to danger instinctually. This can be useful, as in the case of avoiding a snarling dog, or even lifesaving by swerving to avoid an oncoming vehicle. But our natural instincts can also prove dangerous when they imperil our ability to make rational financial decisions.

These behaviors, emotions and biases exist in everyone. We all face contingencies that test our ability to stay calm, tune out distractions and avoid destructive behavior when making decisions about our financial future.

Our goal as advisors is to help our clients pursue their financial objectives while weathering the uncertainties of life and the markets. We are here to listen, understand and share our clients' values and help them transition from working into retirement.

Overcoming Biases

One of the principal reasons for creating a comprehensive plan is to help you avoid making biased financial decisions. Most individuals are unaware that their decisions are influenced by emotions and biases, but they affect virtually every investor in one way or another.

The tendency to use mental shortcuts — feelings rather than logic — to make decisions or solve problems is called a heuristic. These can be helpful or detrimental, depending on whether they produce a correct judgment. When they don't, a bias emerges — a mismatch between judgment and reality.

A significant amount of research and analysis of biases has been done in the field of behavioral finance, specifically, why investors make irrational financial decisions. University of Chicago professors Richard Thaler and Nicholas Barberis have pioneered much of the work, as have Hersh Shefrin and Nobel Prize winner Daniel Kahneman, all of whom have provided substantive background on a variety of biases that tend to impair investor judgment. The following represent a small sampling of the array of biases that can threaten investor judgment and decisions. There are many others, but these are the behaviors that affect the majority of investors.

Hindsight Bias

A Hindsight Bias causes investors to believe they knew beforehand that a stock would go up or down in value; the "I knew it all along" phenomenon. Hindsight investors selectively recall information consistent with what they now know to be true. Psychologists describe it as the tendency to overestimate one's ability to have predicted an outcome that could not possibly have been predicted.

According to Neal Roese, professor of marketing at the Kellogg School of Management at Northwestern University, "The important thing to know about hindsight bias is that it not only changes how you see the world, but also how you see yourself in it. You begin to think: 'Hey, I'm good. I'm really good at figuring out what's going to happen.' You begin to see outcomes as inevitable that were not."

Financial news hosts function as Monday quarterbacks: once the closing bell rings, they tell you the reasons why the market was up or down today. Hindsight is always right, of course. The prognostications of media "guest analysts" are equally worthless. When they are occasionally right, they reappear to take credit for their predictions; when wrong, their miscalculations are ignored. Right or wrong, the same cast of characters will be back to guess again.

Mental Accounting

When an investor views various sources of money as being different from others, it's called Mental Accounting. Money earned from working may be perceived differently than money won gambling or from an inheritance.

A widow we know has a retirement portfolio heavily overweighed with a single stock. She refuses suggestions to diversify her holdings by liquidating some of the stock because it was the favorite stock of her late husband, who preached that she should never sell the security. She was too attached to that memory to recognize the inherent risk of being so poorly diversified. This same problem often arises with employees holding a disproportionate amount of their employer's stock in a 401k.

Individuals expecting a tax refund often talk about what they plan to do with the "extra" money, as if it were a different type of currency to be spent only on luxuries, vacations or other discretionary purchases. Their mental accounting bias distorts their perception of money. Earnings pay bills; tax refunds fund entertainment.

Loss Aversion

Investors with a Loss Aversion bias suffer greater anxiety over losses than they delight in gains. They dislike losing more than they like winning. In their 2008 book, "Sway: The Irresistible Pull of Irrational Behavior," researchers Ori and Rom Brafman state that athletic teams often play to avoid losing, rather than to win.

Loss aversion causes investors to perceive a loss as larger than a gain of the same amount. The bias fuels inaction over action and the status quo over any alternatives.

"Loss aversion is a powerful conservative force that favors minimal changes from the status quo in the lives of both institutions and individuals."

Daniel Kahneman,
"Thinking Fast and Slow."

Herding

Herding occurs when an investor makes choices based on group behaviors rather than deciding independently on the basis of his own information. Interestingly, the bias is not limited to individuals. Institutions herd as much or even more than individuals in that investments chosen by one institution tend to mimic or predict the investment choices of other institutions. Investors extrapolate recent events into the indefinite future. They make predictions based on unfounded conclusions about what has previously occurred.

The tech bubble of the 90's is a classic example of herding. Fueled by irrational exuberance, individuals and institutional investors alike ignored both fundamentals and the historical certainty that a plunge was inevitable. Like the 70's Nifty Fifty, otherwise intelligent people acted like lemmings and followed the group over the cliff.

John Maynard Keynes conceived herding as a response to uncertainty and individuals' perceptions of their own ignorance: people may follow the crowd because they think that the rest of the crowd is better informed. He observed that it is better to be conventionally wrong than unconventionally right because following may help individuals maintain their good reputation and it makes sense to follow the crowd because there is safety in numbers.[10]

Buy! Sell! Cartoon by cartoonist Kevin Kallaugher, Kaltoons.com.

Keynes used the beauty contest as a metaphor for the reasoning that characterizes financial speculation. Competitors in a newspaper contest were asked to choose from a series of photos — not who they thought was the most beautiful but who they thought the others would think most beautiful. Keynes argued that a similar process describes financial speculation. Investors will purchase an exotic automobile, luxury home or perceived hot stock at an obviously inflated price, not because they believe the item is worth the price but because they believe other people will think it is.

The CFA Institute conducted a survey of 724 financial practitioners, asking them to select the behavioral bias that affects investment decisions the most. Graphic 1.2 reveals that herding garnered 34% of the votes and was the topmost bias affecting investment decision making in the eyes of poll participants.[11]

Which of the following behavioral biases affects investment decision making the most?)

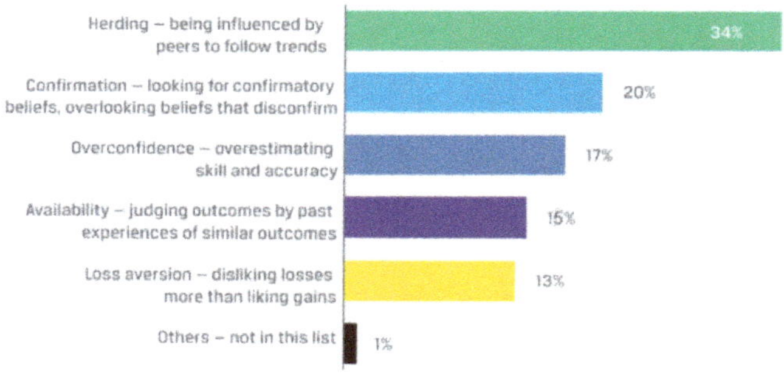

Source: CFA Institute

One of the more fascinating aspects of herding involves the differences between the emotional and analytical sides of our brains. Various studies indicate that modern man's emotional brain tends to be more developed than his analytical brain for reasons dating back to caveman days. When cavemen heard a roar, the emotional cavemen would immediately run for cover whereas the analytical cavemen would stop to consider various factors before deciding whether they needed to run or not. Was the noise was coming from a Tyrannosaurus Rex or a plant eater? If from a carnivorous dinosaur, what time of day is it? Has he already eaten? Am I downwind or upwind? Sooner or later, their analysis would be wrong and they would be eaten.

Those who ran — the emotional cavemen — survived and ultimately became our ancestors. That survival instinct remains hardwired in our DNA today. It prompts us to run from danger. Every time the stock market plunges, our emotional brain kicks in and tells us to run from danger and so that's what we do.

Another aspect of herding that researchers believe may be traced back to our caveman ancestors is the tendency to follow the crowd. That's because if you were part of a prehistoric village or group and ignored the group ethic, you were shunned or kicked out and that meant automatic death. So while there may have been some things you didn't agree with, you just went along with the group program because you wanted to survive.

Today, investors often follow the crowd right through to the calamitous end of a bubble because they fear being shunned or ostracized. The overdeveloped emotional side of our brain can get us into trouble.

Affect

In Psychology, the term affect means emotional feeling, while Shefrin describes the affect heuristic as "the tendency of making decisions based on intuition, instinct and gut feeling." Intuition can be valuable, as can experience, but they are poor substitutes for careful analysis of factual information. Nevertheless, relying on emotions or feelings can appear to be an easier and seemingly more efficient way to make judgments about the complexities of the markets. Dalbar studies reveal that the average investor historically makes significantly less than their index benchmarks. The problem does not appear to be fund performance but rather that investors, acting on emotion or feelings, switch in and out of funds too frequently and at the wrong times. Here are some startling numbers from Dalbar research[12].

For the year 2016, the S&P 500 annualized return was 11.96% but the average equity fund investor return was just 7.26%. The S&P annualized return for the previous 30 years was 10.16%, but again, the average equity fund investor underperformed at only 3.98%, a significant difference.[13]

"With careful and prolonged planning, we may reduce or eliminate many potential sources of bias, but seldom will we be able to eliminate all of them. Accept bias as inevitable and then endeavor to recognize and report all exceptions that do slip thought the cracks."

Good and Hardin, Common Errors in Statistics

Your Outcome

The financial markets reflect the irrational behaviors and collective biases of investors who allow their emotions to dictate their financial decisions. Most do not recognize they are being controlled by emotions that lead to poor choices and bad outcomes.

You do not have to be one of the victims of this phenomenon. If you are aware of your emotional biases, you can control them and avoid the pitfalls they create for so many others.

Humans are emotional beings. Like you, we are emotional people. As advisors, we experience the same emotions you do when the market drops precipitously. Although we also recognize that our reactions are rooted in our ancestors and how they reacted to perceived or real dangers.

The emotional side of our brain is more highly developed than the analytical side.

Like us, you must learn to control your ancestral reactions to perceived danger, the emotions that feel natural but endanger your financial future. To do that, you need a reliable roadmap of the emotional journey you're going to experience during your working years and into and throughout retirement. You need a solid plan and a process you can trust on your journey. You're still going to experience emotions because you're human. Events with the potential to derail your plan may occur: illness, accidents, career setbacks, death of a family member. Things may happen but a good plan and a dependable process will help you pursue your goals by providing a contingency for the unforeseen as well as the predictable, while alleviating unnecessary stress along the way.

Chapter Eight

Estate Planning Errors

Estate planning, perhaps the most complex area of financial planning, means different things to different people. The majority of our clients view estate planning as a seamless process that aims to preserve their assets, ensure adequate lifetime income and enjoy the transition of their legacy to their family, charities or other interests.

In addition to pursuing these goals, estate planning should bring a family together. That doesn't always happen, however. We've seen divorces among heirs triggered by inherited money. We've seen simple errors or oversights cause heartbreaking consequences. Too often, the outcome of an estate plan has little resemblance to the intentions of the benefactor.

Not knowing what you don't know can bring about unintended — and sometimes disastrous — consequences. While a comprehensive discussion of all the things that can go wrong could be a book in itself, what follows is an overview of some of the most common errors we have seen in our combined four decades of doing estate planning.

Procrastination — or Not Having an Estate Plan

A lot of people delay creating an estate plan because of an unwarranted fear of talking about late life issues. It's almost as if avoiding the discussion will somehow prevent aging and death from happening. Sometimes, it's simply a matter of people being busy with their lives. They see estate planning as something that eventually needs to be done but gets put off in favor of more pressing events. Many families find it difficult to have multigenerational conversations about estate planning issues. Children might be uncomfortable talking about the end of their parent's lives.

Another reason for procrastination is that people have a fear of making mistakes and so delay doing what needs to be done. This can have tragic repercussions when a sudden death, disability or permanent incapacity occurs.

Even with what appears to be careful planning, things can go wrong. In one family, a maternal grandmother died, leaving a house and roughly $50,000 in other assets to her three children. One of the children's spouses removed a sewing machine from the home without asking. While not exactly an heirloom, the machine held special memories for the daughter, who learned how to sew from her mother using the machine. The three children stopped talking to one another for the next ten years over the removal of that inexpensive but treasured appliance.

When planning their estate, we try to get our clients to include their children early on when it comes to discussing those few items that might not have great monetary value but are worth a great deal from a sentimental perspective. The distribution of those items should be discussed ahead of time, while everyone is alive and cognizant. Seemingly trivial items or matters can cause major arguments. The overwhelming wish of most clients is that the assets they leave to their children should not cause problems.

We had a situation recently involving three financially secure siblings. One sister who was especially secure retired early so she could relocate to Florida to take care of their father, who was in ill health. She spent the next two years tending to her dying parent, who established a trust and named her executor of his estate. Together, they did all the proper planning. He decided that because she was the only single sibling, she would receive half the assets with the other half split evenly between his two married children. Ironically, the daughter felt uncomfortable with the arrangement and planned to divvy up the assets equally with her two siblings, but before she could do so, the other two expressed such distrust and animosity towards her that the three now hardly speak to one another. The father's wishes may or may not have been the wisest thing to do, but because they were never discussed while he was alive, he put his most devoted child in a bind after his death and caused the other two children to feel as though they were cheated. The more communication you can have about your final wishes early on, the better. It may be an uneasy activity for you and other family members, but the knowledge that you will be minimizing the chances for internal conflict after your death should be ample reason to insist on a family meeting. Estate planning has many meanings, not the least of which is honest and timely communication about your late life wishes. It's not just about creating documents.

On a personal note, one of our mothers grew up with very little in the way of creature comforts. My grandfather died when my mom was a teenager, leaving little beyond a $5,000 life insurance policy, which my grandmother used to purchase a modest house. My grandmother remarried and subsequently passed away. Her second husband then remarried to a person the family frequently referred to as the "war witch". He sold the house — that had appreciated significantly — and moved into his new wife's house. He used the proceeds from the sale of the original house to remodel his new wife's home, doubling its size. He quickly discovered his mistake in marrying the woman and divorced her. In addition to receiving half his pension, the war witch did not have to pay back any of the money he invested in her home remodel, which represented my grandmother's original life insurance money. This happened because the family didn't do the proper estate planning and legal work. There was so little money at the time the patriarch died that estate planning didn't even occur to the family. It was a small mistake that became a nightmare. A not very nice woman wound up with the bulk of the enlarged estate as a result of a divorce and lack of planning. Nobody intends this sort of thing but it happens all the time.

Improper Trust Decisions

Who is going to be responsible for managing your final affairs? It's a critical decision, one with potentially dire consequences if made arbitrarily. Many people randomly name their oldest child as executor of their estate, for no reason other than he or she was the first born. The choice should be based on who is best qualified to handle the task and most likely to see that your wishes are carried out. If no one in the immediate family fills the requirements — or if no one appears to want the job — it may be wise to choose a financial professional as trustee. You may prefer to have your spouse or child to act as trustee, but if they don't have the time or knowledge to handle the responsibility, you can avoid family angst and individual stress by naming a carefully vetted outside trustee.

The person or people chosen to administer an estate has numerous responsibilities, including assembling the assets, paying obligations and distributing the remaining assets to beneficiaries. On the surface, this may seem like a relatively simple process but in actuality, these tasks can be highly complex, time consuming, and in some cases, technically demanding.

Selecting a beneficiary as executor can result in a conflict of interest. That person may be forced to choose between personal interests and those of the other beneficiaries. Selecting a business associate may also result in a conflict of interest if the executor's job is to decide whether or not to sell the business interest or to obtain the highest possible sales price. Sometimes the selected executor has neither the time nor the inclination to devote to the sometimes long and drawn out process of estate administration. Lastly, the appointment of executors who do not know or get along well with family members sometimes results in chaos.[14]

Not Keeping Everything Updated

Failing to update documents or retitle assets can eliminate expected estate planning benefits. One common mistake is to neglect changing beneficiary designations when necessary. Circumstances tend to change over time, as do tax laws; your estate plan should change with them.

Many changes can occur within a family: births, deaths, divorces, remarriages. It makes sense to regularly review your will to ensure the assets you leave behind are given to those you intend.

We frequently see examples where beneficiaries are not updated in current or previous employer retirement plans, life insurance policies or pension plans. In some instances, a person with children divorces, does not remarry, passes away, and the former spouse gets the assets instead of the children.

Poor Communication with the Executor or Beneficiaries

It can drive the executor crazy — and cost thousands of dollars of expenses — if estate and financial documents are difficult or impossible to find because people hide assets, such as cash. Many survivors have never been told what the decedent's goals were, what assets they can rely on for income or capital needs, or how best to utilize the available resources. Many widows or surviving children never had a meaningful discussion with the decedent about their financial security if something were to happen.[15]

Larger estates can involve rivalry and envy among beneficiaries. It's not at all uncommon for heirs to waste the entire value of the estate fighting over what someone else inherited. At that point, the estate and the family relationships are gone.

Talking about death and dying is not something that comes naturally to most families. But communicating your plans and the intentions behind them could prevent estate planning mistakes and save everyone heartache and money.[16]

One of our distant relatives, an aunt, passed away and had entrusted the key to her bank safety box to her two elderly nieces. The aunt had run a small restaurant and lived frugally. When the ladies went to their aunt's bank and opened her safety deposit box, they discovered over one million in cash inside. The banker told them they couldn't touch the money and went to get his boss. It was winter, and as soon as the banker left, the two elderly women began stuffing cash into every available pocket. When the banker returned with his VP, he commented that he thought there was more money in the box but, not wanting to cause a scene, allowed the ladies to leave, each of them several pounds heavier than when they entered the bank. The point is the aunt had left no plan or specific instructions regarding the money. Whatever she might have intended for the money, the two nieces took matters in their own hands and were free to do whatever they wanted with it. That might not have been what the aunt had wished.

Summary

No one gets out of life alive but thoughtful dialogue between parents and children can be one of the most important conversations a family will ever have. Knowing your personal and financial wishes will be properly carried out when your life comes to a conclusion can be a source of great comfort.

Chapter Nine

Women and Money in Motion

While women and men encounter many of the same financial issues, today's women face a new and unique set of challenges.

Overall, an increasing number of today's women — whether married or single — are more actively involved in financial planning and investment decisions, a positive development.

Many of our clients are women, some of whom earn substantial incomes. Some readily embrace financial decision-making; others have it thrust upon them due to death or divorce.

Because of our commitment and many years of experience helping women successfully plan and invest for their futures, we've acquired a deeper understanding of both the financial and emotional obstacles they must overcome.

The "What if's"

Women we work with recognize the importance of having a clear financial plan. They also understand the need to consider the "what if's" — the unexpected events that can derail the plan. For example, what if she becomes unemployed? Will she be alright until she finds another position? Will she be able to retire and maintain her lifestyle? Statistically, women live longer than men. If married, what if her husband dies unexpectedly?

One of the things we occasionally notice in meeting with married couples is that the husband might ask simply, "Are we good?" If we reply, "Yes, we're good," he is satisfied. The wife, however, will want to know more. Women tend to be more concerned with details and understanding the long-term picture whereas men tend to assume everything will be fine. This is obviously not always the case but it is not uncommon.

A Personal Comment

Our three wives are all bright women who have chosen to raise families rather than continue their professional careers. Fortunately, we are all doing well and because we are financial advisors, our wives tend to delegate investment and retirement planning decisions to us. It's not that they aren't interested or capable of managing financial matters; they trust us to make smart choices and simply want to know that they and the children will be okay should something happen to us.

Non-Participating Wives

People who marry nowadays typically see themselves as teammates. They may divide responsibilities but both are actively — and equally — involved in important decisions.

One or the other may take the reins of the couple's financial future, but it's by agreement, not appropriation. This is especially true of dual income couples. We believe it's fine to have this type of arrangement, assuming both parties agree, but at least once a year we recommend both spouses meet with their advisor to review their financial picture. Wives tend to live longer than their husbands; we don't want them to wake up one day as widows not knowing anything about their financial future. How do these women protect themselves financially should they divorce or become widows?

Spouses that don't participate in financial matters or have a relationship with a financial advisor may, upon becoming a widow, feel pressure to make hurried decisions about financial matters. They may be predisposed to asking friends or family members lacking financial expertise for advice. Equally troubling, they may rely on the advice of an advisor lacking the necessary tax, retirement, estate planning or other specific knowledge applicable to their situation. Worse, they may become victims of financial con artists who prey on widows, seniors and those under duress.

Bob and Julie were married for 20+ years, each earning six-figure incomes when they divorced. Bob had always handled the couple's financial affairs while Julie preferred to focus on cooking and decorating. Fifteen years after the divorce, Julie continues to suffer anxiety about her financial future, despite her substantial income and retirement savings. It's not uncommon for even highly compensated career women to experience angst about investments, taxes, pensions and other financial complications after a divorce. That torment may continue indefinitely without compassionate advisory counsel.

Unplanned Singles

The term "unplanned singles" refers to women who unexpectedly become single as the result of a divorce or spousal death. The emotional trauma associated with either event can make rational decision-making difficult, if not impossible.

Some worrisome statistics regarding widowhood:

- Women are three times more likely than men to become widowed[1]
- About one-fourth of women who become widows are under age 65[2]
- On average, widowhood itself causes a 37% decline in income for a woman and a 22% decline for a man[3]
- Roughly 17% of widows aged 55 and older live below the poverty line[4]

Widows may be confronted with a number of tasks related to the death of their spouse. Gathering financial records, insurance policies, retirement assets and other necessary paperwork can be an onerous chore, particularly while grieving. If the widow was not actively involved in the couple's financial decisions, getting through the process can be a terrifying experience. The widow may not only have difficulty locating everything needed to expedite the financial transition — where did Phil keep his 401k records from previous employers? — she may not be able to differentiate what is important from what is insignificant. The knowledge and understanding of an experienced advisory team can be invaluable for the widow, but if she never participated in financial planning sessions or investment discussions, who does she turn to in her time of need?

Even when a wife doesn't have much interest in financial matters, it's important for her to participate, at least occasionally, in meetings with the couple's financial advisor. The last thing we want as advisors is to have a widow sitting in front of us, frightened that she might be getting bad advice because she never came to the couple's financial meetings and so doesn't have an established trust relationship with us the way her husband did.

If you are a married woman who divides up the tasks or one that doesn't have an interest in finances and investments, get involved...force yourself to attend financial meetings with your advisor so you get to know them as someone you will feel comfortable with in case something happens to your spouse. Build a relationship; it's worth the effort.

We share that commentary with our married clients if one spouse (usually the wife) isn't coming along to our meetings at least once a year so she gets to know us. We tell the husband, if something happens to you, we don't want her in that situation.

Of course, a whole different set of emotions surface during divorce where rational thinking may be clouded more by anger than by loss.

Jean was raised in an upper-income household, attended private schools and enjoyed all the advantages her parent's wealth could provide. In her early twenties, she married a successful alpha male who similarly provided her with virtually anything she desired. Essentially, Jean lived like someone with a money tree in her backyard.

Shortly after the last of her three children graduated from college, Jean's husband announced he wanted a divorce. It proved to be a contentious process that took nearly five years to adjudicate. Recognizing that Jean wasn't financially astute and fearing she might eventually run out of money, the husband wanted to structure the divorce payout but Jean resisted. He owned his own business but the couple was unable to agree on its value so it became necessary for the husband to sell it so they could divide the assets.

Jean remained bitter and began spending the substantial settlement money as though nothing had changed and that tree in her backyard was still sprouting money. She seemed unable to come to terms with life being different. Her children were alarmed about her reckless spending and refusal to change her behavior, fearing she would eventually go broke and become financially dependent on them.

The children asked us to intervene so we arranged a meeting with them and Jean. We explained that her anger and inability to rein in her spending would ultimately result in her running out of money. The concept of not having unlimited funds had never occurred to her, perhaps not surprising given her history. What she needed was a plan to help preserve what remained of her settlement capital while simultaneously seeking to provide income. To this day, she remains bitter but has learned to live on a reasonable budget...and her children are relieved.

Depending on their upbringing and other circumstances, people regard money differently. Jean transitioned from having mom and dad providing for her to having a successful husband doing the same. For the first 50 years of her life, she only had to ask for what she wanted and her request was fulfilled. Once divorced, she adopted the attitude that she would now have to take care of herself, but she didn't change her spending habits.

When we become advisor to people like Jean, our primary objective is to avoid having them run out of money. This type of situation occurs more often than you might expect.

Caretakers

One of the more difficult situations arises when a woman who doesn't have a role in the family's finances discovers that her husband is losing competency. It's an awkward dynamic when the husband who has always been in charge of financial matters is no longer capable of making sound decisions but the wife doesn't want to embarrass him. We've conducted client meetings where the husband still insists on making financial decisions when it's apparent, he is not able to do so. What often happens is the wife pulls us aside when the husband goes to the washroom and asks what she can do. It can be heartbreaking to see a woman who is a caretaker frustrated when she has no previous experience.

A complication related to the caretaker role involves women who are caring for an older family member as well as themselves. They might be a younger woman dealing with a dementia husband or parent, or a child with severe learning disabilities. It can be an enormous burden and they may have no one outside the immediate family with whom to communicate their difficulties. We've encountered instances where a woman is taking care of four generations: aging parents, their own family, their children, and their grandchildren. In some cases, they're taking on the burden alone.

One of the conversations we try to have with new clients in these types of situations is to allow us to become their navigator. We help them get organized and determine what to do and where to go. They have so many issues and need a plan that allows them to see light at the end of the tunnel. Sometimes, these women prefer we take the reins; other times, they want to remain directly involved in every step as we go through the process. What's important is to understand their needs, alleviate their stress and find a path forward that they can trust. They engage us to help soften the burden they've been carrying all on their own.

In cases where they have a son or daughter who can be trusted to help with the finances, we try to include them. A lot of women don't realize that's an option and express appreciation that we thought to include their children in the solution.

Pension Issues

A divorced woman was referred to a financial advisor friend by her son, who sought to help his mother with some tax and pension considerations. The advisor was a college roommate of the son and the two had continued their friendship after graduation. Unfortunately, the advisor, who earned his living selling insurance products, lacked experience with the issues the divorced woman faced. When she told him she wanted to pay off the mortgage on her home, he suggested she withdraw $200,000 from her 401k. The action triggered a near $100,000 taxable event.

Getting advice from a "financial professional" who is unfamiliar with the tax ramifications of the pension rollover process can wreak havoc with the finances of a divorcee or widow.

We have been involved in several divorce situations where both the existing advisors and the divorcees were unsure how to interpret pensions, stock options and other financial issues that could have a profound impact on the funds available to them. Mistakes involving tax issues alone can significantly reduce the size of the pot. Understanding the value of pensions is rarely intuitive. Steering divorcees through the obstacles that could imperil their financial futures is not an exercise for financial neophytes or attorneys. In addition to retirement benefit issues, other financial considerations in a divorce include property settlements, spousal and child support, tax implications, joint debts, health and life insurance, prenuptial agreements and Social Security options. Having an experienced advisor to help guide divorcees on how to equalize assets can make all the difference.

We helped a couple who were divorcing after 40 years. The stumbling block in the negotiations were the couple's assets. One spouse had a financial perspective; the other a more emotional viewpoint. Of course, the two are not equal and it created an awkward and complicated situation. We calculated the present and future value of the assets' income stream to help clarify the complexities of the arrangement but the emotional partner resisted, angry over having to go through a divorce and now having to try to understand a complex financial concept. The present value of an income stream is not the easiest concept to explain or understand. It requires patience on the part of an advisor and an understanding of the emotional as well as financial needs of both parties. It's an important balancing act that the financial advisor often has to work through with divorcing clients.

Recap

A host of emotions can surface as a result of divorce or death. When meeting with women in these situations, we understand the gamut of emotions they are going through. We explore their concerns, the issues that trouble them most, and seek practical approaches to dealing with and eventually overcoming the impediments to their future wellbeing. In some cases, they may not be aware of what the issues are or why they are experiencing such overwhelming emotional trauma, which is why they need someone knowledgeable and objective to guide them through the process.

The best financial planners — professionals who may have all the technical knowledge regarding issues related to death and divorce — can fail their clients if they can't muster the patience and compassion needed in these situations. Before an advisor's financial competence comes into play, his or her experience and listening skills are of paramount importance. When a woman is undergoing a spouse's death or divorce, and especially where sizeable money in motion is involved, an advisor's listening skills and reassurance can be critical.

Chapter 10

Finding a Competent Advisor

A thought struck me while watching an NBA championship game. One of the players was making shot after shot, most of which were from 25 or 30 feet away. He was "in the zone" and it seemed like he didn't even have to aim; he just tossed the ball up and in it went. He could hardly wait to get his hands on the ball and hoist up another swish. He obviously felt he couldn't miss. Interestingly, during his previous game, that same player missed 15 consecutive shots, experiencing one of his worst-ever shooting nights.

Sometimes, the markets are like that. Since sinking to the depths in 2009, the DJIA has had a remarkable rebound, tripling in value through the end of 2016.[17] The happy result is that virtually anyone who remained invested has been "in the zone" for the past decade. Advisors and investment managers are once again gleefully touting their performance. The market has been on such a roll, even do-it-yourself investors have temporarily overcome their inherent tendencies to self-destruct.

It's been such a great run that an increasing number of people have become convinced they can successfully manage their own investments. The combination of an extended bull market, easy access to financial information and the emergence of discount brokerage has spawned a horde of self-confident DIY investors. It's a trend with potentially disastrous consequences.

Just as everyone thinks they are a competent driver, when the market is peaking, everyone thinks they are competent at choosing investments. The reality is another story, however.

As previously cited, Dalbar's 2016 Quantitative Analysis of Investor Behavior (QAIB), illustrates how poorly the average investor does when compared with S&P 500 index (see chart 10.1). Over extended periods of 10, 20 and 30 years, average investors consistently underper-form both equity returns as measured by the S&P 500 and fixed income returns as measured by the Barclay's Aggregate Bond Index.

	Investor Returns					
	Equity Funds	Asset Allocation Funds	Fixed Income Funds	Inflation	S&P 500	Barclays Aggregate Bond Index
30 Year	3.66	1.65	0.59	2.60	10.35	6.73
20 Year	4.67	2.11	0.51	2.20	8.19	5.37
10 Year	4.23	1.89	0.39	1.88	7.31	4.51
5 Year	6.92	3.28	0.10	1.58	12.57	3.25
3 Year	8.85	3.81	-1.76	1.07	15.13	1.44
12 Months	-2.28	-3.48	-3.11	0.95	1.38	0.55

Returns are for the period ending December 31, 2015. Average equity investor, average bond investor and average asset allocation investor performance results are calculated using data supplied by the Investment Company Institute. Investor returns are represented by the change in total mutual fund assets after excluding sales, redemptions and exchanges. This method of calculation captures realized and unrealized capital gains, dividends, interest, trading costs, sales charges, fees, expenses and any other costs. After calculating investor returns in dollar terms, two percentages are calculated for the period examined: Total investor return rate and annualized investor return rate. Total return rate is determined by calculating the investor return dollars as a percentage of the net of the sales, redemptions and exchanges for each period.

When investors start to think, "this time it's different," they are headed for trouble. The history of the financial markets teaches us that nothing continues indefinitely and nothing is as sure as change. Every upsurge is eventually followed by a decline and vice versa. The problem for many investors — especially DIYers — is that they get in or out of the market at precisely the wrong time. Their emotions take control of their decision-making and they end up doing the opposite of what is best for their portfolio.

One of the main reasons for engaging professional help is having an experienced voice of reason to help you avoid kneejerk reactions and to guide you through turbulent markets. Of course, that assumes you have chosen your advisor wisely. There are a number of questions to ask that should help you determine if you have the right person to guide you to your financial goals. There are also a number of red flags that should warn you to look elsewhere.

What to Look For

First and foremost, you want someone who is honest. We believe most advisors are fundamentally honest, but you must find an investment advisor dedicated to working in your best interests, not those of the advisor. If the advisor promises returns far above the market average, beware: they are likely too good to be true.

Legitimate investments are structured for the long run. Watch out for the advisor who claims to have access to "hot stocks" or who touts investment opportunities that must be acted upon quickly. These are warning signs; walk away.

There has been a lot of discussion recently regarding the fiduciary standard. The description of a fiduciary is often oversimplified so as to reassure investors. Wikipedia defines it thusly: "A fiduciary is a person who holds a legal or ethical relationship of trust with one or more other parties (person or group of persons). Typically, a fiduciary prudently takes care of money or other assets for another person."

If only it were that simple. For example, an advisor may serve as fiduciary to the client, the investment account or their employer. Just because an advisor says he or she is a fiduciary is in of itself no guarantee they will act in your best interest. They may be held to a fiduciary standard for their employer, not you.

Advisors running ethical practices always put their clients' needs first, in effect, meeting a fiduciary standard. A Certified Financial Planner™ is a professional that follows a fiduciary standard to his or her clients, as defined by the CFP Board. This responsibility holds them to a higher standard of ethical behavior. In this regard, a Certified Financial Planner™ will look for specific factors when investing to ensure your investments are managed in your best interests. This standard includes allocating assets based on your expressed needs and goals; identifying sources of risk and initiating a strategy to manage exposure; and minimizing tax liability associated with individual and business investments, and addressing other relevant issues.

Fees

You should clearly understand how much you will be charged and the way you will be charged for services from your investment advisor. Of course, your advisor deserves to be paid, but if your advisor won't give you a concise answer regarding fees and other associated costs, you need to find an advisor who will.

While there are different fee structures, some models can raise some red flags. Do the transaction fees seem excessive? Rather than help you, some investment advisors help themselves by engaging in multiple transactions to generate commissions.

The advisor should be transparent in the fees assessed to you as a client. You may be paying a fee to your advisor and also a fee to the underlying investment. Together these multiple costs add up and can eat away at your wealth accumulation.

Staff or Solo?

Another consideration is whether the advisor has adequate support or works alone. Today, it's virtually impossible to oversee financial planning, investment management, taxes and estate planning and — by the way, also oversee running a business — without having a skilled support team to delegate to. You don't want to trust the complexities of your financial future to someone working alone.

Occasionally we hear from someone who met with an advisor at a major brokerage firm or one of the "name" companies and assumed all the people in that office worked together. Most of the time, that's not the case. Most of those advisors are solo practitioners who share office space with everyone else in the place. They're all in competition. The advisor they're meeting with will likely be the only person working on their account.

The perceived prestige of the major brokerage firms is largely a result of huge advertising campaigns. They create the impression that clients receive an elevated level of expertise and access to enormous resources when, typically, that's simply not true unless they have multimillion dollar portfolios. The average investor does not get that kind of concierge service. They get access to solo practitioners who are trying to market to prospects, meet and service clients, build and oversee client portfolios and address client planning issues, all as a one-person team. Their brokerage firm may have additional resources available but the solo practitioner likely has no time to tap into those resources.

A good question to ask prospective advisors is how many people they actually employ. Ambiguous references to "team members" by advisors who are essentially sole practitioners have little meaning or value. Advisors at big-name firms may talk about being backed by a "client specialist support team" of analysts and financial specialists but not know how or have the opportunity to use them. You want to work with an advisor who employs other financial specialists with complementary capabilities: <u>people who know you</u>, your situation and your goals.

Our firm has an investment committee meeting every month. We review investment ideas and strategies with a group of knowledgeable people and through that process, we believe we receive better investment advice than a single practitioner interpreting the data. In addition to our firm's principals, we employ a financial planning professional who analyzes our recommendations, so we have several sets of eyes reviewing each client's unique circumstances versus one person feeding data into a computer and coming up with a strategy.

Designations

Some advisors have a string of cryptic acronyms following their name. Most are inconsequential when it comes to establishing meaningful advisory credentials. The Wall Street Journal published an "Alphabet Soup" listing of the several hundred designations available. [18] The "certifications" include many available with just a few hours of online or self-study. There are even some impressive designations available that require no study or testing whatsoever.

When assessing advisor certifications, you should first consider what you need in an advisor. Are you looking for a comprehensive financial planner or someone to manage your investments or an annuity or insurance specialist?

If you're looking for a comprehensive financial planner, the Certified Financial Planner® (CFP) designation indicates that the advisor has completed extensive training and experience requirements and is held to rigorous ethical standards. They are qualified to create comprehensive financial plans and know how to make recommendations in your best interest. They help you analyze all aspects of your financial and personal life and create a plan based on your needs and objectives. Investments will naturally be a piece of the plan, as will tax planning, risk management and transition planning for the next generation.

A caveat: just because someone has achieved the CFP designation does not necessarily mean they are experts at financial planning; it does indicate they have invested the time and expense to acquire the fundamental knowledge, however. It also indicates they have agreed to adhere to a stricter standard of professional ethics and client service. A responsible CFP who determines that you need additional insurance may refer you to an insurance specialist. Similarly, if the plan reveals you have unique tax issues, the CFP can either refer you to a CPA or work harmoniously with your existing accountant. The CFP will act as quarterback of your advisory team, referring issues to specialists when necessary.

This is not to demean financial professionals who lack the CFP designation. For example, there are many trustworthy, competent insurance professionals who will openly reveal that they are life insurance specialists exclusively. The ones you want to avoid are insurance people who portray themselves as comprehensive financial advisors.

Longevity

It's important to select an advisor who has experienced more than one economic cycle; someone who has guided investors through both up and down markets. Obviously, managing investments when the markets are soaring is much easier than helping you remain calm and stay the course when markets are plunging. As mentioned, you need a voice of reason when things get chaotic. That reassurance can only come from an advisor who has already been through a down market and knows what to expect and what to recommend.

When meeting with an advisor for the first time, most people want to talk about investments and investment returns. Sound financial planning is about much more than investments, however. While investments are an important piece of the puzzle, so are taxes, insurance and budgeting, even though clients may not enjoy talking about them. When a client dies and we meet with the widow, the planning we did with the couple years before becomes far more important than the specific investment products chosen or the precise return on those investments.

That's another reason why DIY investors tend to do less well than those with a competent advisor. When we meet with a new client, we ask what kind of investor they are — conservative, aggressive, etc. Once we review their investments, we discover the overwhelming majority have a portfolio that indicates an entirely different investment approach. In some cases, people are simply kidding themselves. Other times, people truly believe they are a conservative investor when their holdings reveal something quite different. As advisors, we spend a lot of time making sure the risk assumptions and financial goals of our clients are aligned with their investments. That's the value of having someone with extensive experience and knowledge guiding you through the obstacle course of planning and investing.

Tell Me The Truth

An advisor should have the confidence to tell you what you need to hear, not what you want to hear. The latter is how many people get into trouble choosing an advisor who is polite, personable and agrees with whatever the client says he or she wants. If an advisor is not strong enough to challenge you when you are misinformed or just plain wrong about something important, you have the wrong advisor. Trust is something that is nurtured and grows over time, but a good rapport is something that should be quickly evident when meeting with an advisor. Capable advisors welcome having tough conversations with their clients even though they're not fun because they uncover details and feelings that are critical to helping the clients work towards the results they hope for. Be wary of the advisor who doesn't challenge you.

Somebody who is out there selling a product or has just one approach isn't going to challenge you. They're going to agree with whatever you say you want and then explain that what they have in their briefcase is exactly what you need.

Just as important as helping you grow your money, your advisor should help you avoid big mistakes. Many times, people do things on their own because they don't think it's important to include their advisor — or don't want their advisor to know what they are doing because they know it may not be a smart decision. The result is often an unintended consequence that can torpedo the best financial plan.

An example comes to mind where an investor surreptitiously made a trade in a nonqualified account. The trade triggered significant capital gains which bumped the investor up past the alternative minimum tax threshold.

In another instance, a retiring executive rolled over the funds from her 401k into her discount brokerage IRA. She didn't know about the 60-day rule and as she was not yet 59.5 years of age, unintentionally created an early distribution. She had to pay regular income tax on the transferred amount in addition to a 10% tax penalty, which amounted to over $50,000.

Working With Your Team

The advisor you choose must be willing to work with your other financial advisors and manage them all with you. Not for you, with you. If an advisor is unwilling to bring your other advisors into the circle and work with them, it's a glaring red flag. No professional should fear having other professionals look at his work. As an advisor, if you're not comfortable having another member of the client's advisory team look at what you're doing, what are you hiding that you don't want them to see? As a client, the more qualified people you can bring into the decision-making process, the better. Bring everyone into the plan so they are all on the same page...assuming you have chosen your advisory team wisely and they are all dedicated to doing what's best for you.

Your advisor should welcome having your CPA, attorney and any other relevant advisors involved in your plans and decisions. In some cases, attorneys and clients will have different discussions than they have with us. There might be something in the past that they told their attorney that they neglect to share with us. The attorney might make a different recommendation than we would by virtue of having that information. If an advisor is doing the right things for you, they should have no issue discussing anything with your other advisors.

Last Word About DIY Investing

There is an adage, "An attorney who represents himself has a fool for a client." When we meet people who tell us they are managing their own portfolio, we ask what they base their investment decisions on and they typically say that they are reading somebody's newsletter or following someone's investment ideas.

If you are paying for someone's advice, how credible is the person you are buying your research from? Like the huckster selling "winners" at the racetrack, just because you are paying for advice doesn't make it good. Financial product marketers such as mutual fund companies can pay brokers to recommend their funds. Financial news shows may invite analysts of brokerage firms with big advertising budgets to appear as "experts." In an interview with Jon Stewart, "Mad Money" host Jim Cramer admitted he is paid for entertainment value, not good advice.

Another disadvantage of DIY is that people tend to pay exclusive attention to the investment equation, ignoring the crucial planning elements that are often more important than investment results. Perhaps the biggest threat for people who do it themselves is that if they die, who is going to take care of their family's financial needs?

Think of yourself as a pilot: if you are flying a plane with your family and you are the only pilot on board and you die, chances are, the plane is going to crash. if you have a copilot on board, your family has a good chance of arriving safely.

The CFP website, www.letsmakeaplan.org has an excellent list of questions to ask a potential advisor. In addition, here are seven key traits you should look for:

Competence: A good financial advisor should be well-educated, and able to demonstrate a significant amount of experience.

Objectivity: Your needs should be at the heart of all your planner's recommendations. Your financial advisor should consider your situation carefully, then give you advice that best addresses your goals. This approach may require your planner to explain that your goals are unrealistic, given current resources and financial commitments.

Integrity: Trust is central to a successful financial planning relationship. You rely on your planner's honesty, professionalism and abilities to help you work towards your goals.

Clarity: Your advisor should be able to state clearly what services will be provided, the costs, the risks associated with their financial recommendations, as well as any potential conflicts of interest. For example, does the financial planner gain personally or financially from your purchase of a particular product or from the outcome of a suggested strategy?

Diligence: Before engaging you as a client, your advisor should discuss your goals and objectives and explain what you can expect from the relationship. A diligent advisor will investigate the products or services they recommend and closely supervise any staff working with you.

Compliance: Your advisor should not offer investment advice or related services unless they are properly qualified and licensed to do so, as required by state or federal law.

Privacy: To get the best results from your advisory relationship, you need to divulge relevant personal and financial information to your advisor. You should expect your adviser to keep this information confidential, sharing it only to conduct business on your behalf and at your consent.

Epilogue

Whether you are a young achiever on your way up, have reached the phase of life where you have accumulated significant wealth, or are in the transition phase prior to retirement, it's not what you know but rather what you don't know that represents the greatest impediment to true financial independence.

As successful businessmen, husbands and fathers, we face the same challenges you do. We contend with the same concerns, emotions and distractions.

We've been there.

We hope in writing this book, you are now better able to recognize and deal with the issues that can prevent you from reaching your goals. We believe this knowledge, applied consistently, can help you make seamless transitions through the various phases of your life.

Keith Mooney and Joe Lyons
Mooney Lyons Financial Services
www.mooneylyons.com

Endnotes

---

[1] July, 2015 estimates by the U.S. Census Bureau.

[2] Decennial Census (1960); American Community Survey (2013).

[3] Meredith Woodward King, "Kids these days' redux: Clark Professor Jeffrey Arnett joins media's 'Millennial pledge' debate," www.clarku.edu 2 Nov 2015.

[4] Ibid.

[5] Phantom stock plans get their name from the hypothetical units that are used within the plan. These units represent "phantom" shares of the company that are assigned to the plan participant and rise and fall in value in tandem with the company share price.

[6] Centers for Disease Control and Prevention's National Center for Health Statistics.hyperactive

[7] Nanci Hellmich, "Retirement: Some struggle with leaving their jobs," USA Today 28 Oct 2014.

[8] Dollar cost averaging involves continuous investment in securities regardless of fluctuation in price levels of such securities. Such a plan does not assure a profit and does not protect against loss in declining markets.

[9] futures.tradingcharts.com/historical/GD/1981/0/continuous.html

[10] Michelle Baddeley, "Herding, social influence and economic decision-making," Philosophical Transactions of The Royal Society Dec 2009.

[11] Shreenivas Kuntr, CFA, "The Herding Mentality: Behavioral Finance and Investor Biases," CFA Institute 6 Aug 2015.

[12] QAIB uses data from the Investment Company Institute (ICI), Standard & Poor's and Barclays Capital Index Products to compare investor returns to an appropriate set of benchmarks. Covering the period from January 1, 1996, to December 31, 2016, the study utilizes mutual fund sales, redemptions and exchanges each month as a measure of investor behavior. Average investor return is based on an analysis by Dalbar Inc., which utilizes the net of aggregate mutual fund sales, redemptions and exchanges each month as a measure of investor behavior. Returns are annualized (and total return where applicable). The S&P 500 is an unmanaged index of 500 widely held stocks that is generally considered representative of the U.S. stock market. Barclays Capital Aggregate Index covers the U.S.. investment grade fixed rate bond market, with index components for government and corporate securities, mortgage pass-through securities, and asset-backed securities.

[13] DALBAR 2016 QAIB: Investors are Still Their Own Worst Enemy.

[14] lifehealthpro.com

[15] ibid

[16] bankrate.com

[17] http://www.macrotrends.net/1358/dow-jones-industrial-average-last-10-years

[18] "Alphabet Soup," The Wall Street Journal 16 Oct 2010.

CPSIA information can be obtained
at www.ICGtesting.com
Printed in the USA
BVHW060836260120
570494BV00001B/2/J

9 781506 905501